Stock Market Investing for Beginners:

Essentials to Start Investing Successfully

Table of Contents

Introduction

Chapter 1: Stocks 101

    What is a stock?
    The stock market
    Is it gambling?
    Short term vs. long term
    The truth behind the myths

        Investing in stocks is a quick and easy way to make money
        Investing in stocks is only for the rich
        To be successful, you need to have special connections
        Investing in stocks will make you an instant millionaire
        Investing in stocks is safe and risk-free
        Investing in stocks will only make you lose all your money

    Risks

        Market risk
        Economic risk
        Legal risk
        Headline risk
        Commodity price risk
        Interest risk and inflation

    Benefits

        Profitable
        Convenient
        You are the boss
        Financial freedom
        It's fun

    Stock trading broker

        Latest reviews
        Banking
        Trading or Investment platform

- Fees
- Minimum and maximum amount per investment
- Mobile feature
- Customer support
- Demo account

Trading psychology

- Greed
- Fear
- Regret
- Overconfidence
- Winning mindset

Chapter 2: Stock Trading Strategies

- **Fundamental analysis**
- **Technical analysis**
- **Averaging down**
- **Growth investing**
- **Value investing**
- **Stock split**
- **Stock mastery**
- **Develop your own**

Chapter 3: Best Practices

- **Research**
- **Start small**
- **Write a trading or investing journal**
- **Cash out**
- **Take a break**
- **Continuous improvement**
- **Diversify your risks**
- **Professional approach**

Chapter 4: Mistakes to Avoid

- **Chasing after your losses**
- **Using an untested strategy**

Relying completely on expert advice
Taking weak trading positions
Being a victim of the 'pump and dump' scheme
Trading aggressively

Conclusion

© Copyright 2018 by _____ - All rights reserved.

The transmission, duplication, or reproduction of any of the following work including specific information will be considered an illegal act irrespective of whether it is done electronically or in print. This extends to creating a secondary or tertiary copy of the work or a recorded copy and is only allowed with the express written consent from the Publisher. All additional rights reserved.

The information in the following pages is broadly considered to be a truthful and accurate account of facts, and as such any inattention, use, or misuse of the information in question by the reader will render any resulting actions solely under their purview. There are no scenarios in which the publisher or the original author of this work can be, in any fashion, deemed liable for any hardship or damages that may befall them after undertaking information described herein. The author does not take any responsibility for inaccuracies, omissions, or errors which may be found therein.

Additionally, the information in the following pages is intended only for informational purposes and should thus be thought of as universal. As befitting its nature, it is presented without assurance regarding its prolonged validity or interim quality. The author of this work is not responsible for any loss, damage, or inconvenience caused as a result of reliance on information as published on, or linked to, this book.

The author of this book has taken careful measures to share vital information about the subject. May its readers acquire the right knowledge, wisdom, inspiration, and succeed.

Introduction

Congratulations on downloading this book and thank you for doing so.

If you want to leave your 8-hour job and be your own boss, or if you simply want to find a way to increase your monthly income, then you should definitely consider investing in the stock market. By trading stocks, you can earn a high amount of income, even a full-time income. Not to mention, you can enjoy and earn all the profits that you can make from the comfort of your home.

Thanks to the convenience of modern technology, you can start investing in stocks with just a few clicks of the mouse. The real challenge lies in picking the right stocks to invest in. The unfortunate truth is that there are so many people who invest stocks without even understanding what they are doing. The activity of successfully investing in stocks for profit takes so much more than just randomly choosing stocks and hoping for a favorable outcome. In order to be successful, you have to learn and master the basics and use effective trading strategies to turn the odds in your favor. Indeed, given the right foundation and understanding, you can turn the stock market into a goldmine of profits.

The following chapters will teach you the ins and outs of investing in stocks for profit:

- Chapter 1 discusses the basics. Learn about what a 'stock is' and how the stock market works, among many others. This chapter will give you the foundation that you need to be successful

- Chapter 2 teaches the amazing stock investing and trading strategies that you can use to turn the odds in your favor

- Chapter 3 lays down the best practices that you should observe to increase your chances of making a profit

- Chapter 4 talks about the mistakes that you should avoid. You should take note of these pitfalls to avoid committing the same mistakes that many other people did

There are plenty of books on this subject on the market, so thanks again for choosing this one! Every effort was made to ensure it is full of as much useful information as possible. Please enjoy!

Chapter 1: Stocks 101

Before we go into the technical aspects of investing or trading stocks, you should first have a good understanding of the basics. The basics will serve as your foundation, which is very important to your success. This is also a good way to know just what you should expect. Let us discuss them one by one:

What is a stock?

The term 'stock' refers to the ownership of a company. It is also referred to as a 'share of stock' or simply 'share.' Once you buy stocks of a company, you become entitled to the rights of ownership of said company, and this includes rights over the company's earnings, assets, and voting rights. Also, the word 'stocks' is just a general term. Stocks have various classifications, such as common stocks, redeemable stocks, treasury stocks, and many others. But, when you hear investors talk about stocks, they almost always refer to 'common stocks.'

The stock market

The 'stock market' refers to the place or platform where stocks are traded. This is where the buying and selling of stocks take place. The stock market also reflects the economic conditions. This is because when the economy is well, the prices of stocks also tend to increase. However, when the economy is not doing well, then the prices of stocks tend to suffer. Hence, a good tip to determine how good or bad a certain economy is doing is by looking at the behavior of the prices of stocks. Now, keep in mind that the prices of stocks do not just move at random. Stocks are owned mostly by businesses. If the business is doing well, then the prices of stocks increase. However, when the business is not doing well, then the prices of stocks tend to decrease. Okay, you might be wondering: "Why do companies offer their stocks to the public?" The reason here is that by offering stocks to the market, companies can finance their business. After all, in order for you to own a stock, you have to pay for it. By offering stocks, companies can accrue the necessary funds for the expansion and further development of the business. After all, money is the lifeblood of a business.

Is it gambling?

"So, is it gambling?" This is something that many people wonder. The reason why this question usually remains unanswered is because that there is no clear-cut answer to it. This depends on how you approach the activity of investing in or trading stocks. If you approach the market by simply relying on guesswork and assuming that luck is on your side, then you are gambling. In this case, investing in stocks becomes a gamble. However, if every action that you make is backed up by solid research and analysis, and if you consider every position you make as an investment decision, then you are investing and not gambling.

Also, just because there are risks involved in this activity that does not mean that it is gambling. After all, everything has its risks. Even businesses have to deal with many risks and challenges. What is important is how you approach it and how you turn that opportunity that you see into actual profit. So, is investing in stocks a gamble? Well, it depends on you. However, as much as this book is concerned, we discourage relying on luck. Do not gamble. In order to increase your chances of attaining success and enjoy a continuous flow of profits, you should take the time and effort to study the market and apply effective strategies.

Short term vs. long term

When you invest in stocks, you are in control of your investment. This means that you can invest in them for as long as you want or for a short period. At some point in the future, if you feel like closing your position to enjoy your profits, then you can easily do so with just a click of the mouse. Investments in stocks can be divided into two classifications: short-term and long-term investments. There is no clear rule to determine what makes an investment short or long. However, many agree that if the investment is held for longer than a year, then that is a long-term investment, while investments that are held for less than a year are considered short-term investments.

There is also what is known as 'day trading.' As the name suggests, this is trading stocks in one trading day. It is a kind of short-term investment. Day traders are active and make multiple trades in a day. When you day trade, you open your positions and close them at the end of the trading day. You can then start with a clean slate the following day, hence, the term 'day trading.'

Now, it should be noted that the prices of stocks do not fluctuate heavily, unless if you invest in penny stocks, which are much riskier. This means that if you only invest for a few days or weeks, then you might barely see any significant changes in the value of your investment. People who engage in short-term trades, like day traders, normally have a high capital, so a small percentage of gain or loss can have a significant impact on their investment.

So, which is better? A short-term or a long-term investment? Well, none is better than the other. It will depend on your approach and the strategy that you will use. So, just do what you think is the best and most suitable for you. If you are just starting out, then you might want to try both and see what happens. Whether you trade for a short-term or a long-term is up to you to decide.

The truth behind the myths

There are various myths related to stock investing. For you to have a better understanding of the stock market and what it means to be an investor, then you have to know the truth behind these myths:

Investing in stocks is a quick and easy way to make money

Although investing in stocks can make you rich, it is not something that you can easily achieve overnight. Keep in mind that the prices of stocks do not fluctuate rapidly. So, do not expect to make a multi-million profit in just one day. Normally, it takes time to earn a significant amount of income when you invest in stocks. If you invest just a few dollars, then it will surely take some time before you can earn your first million. It is also not easy to make money by investing in stocks since it takes time and considerable effort for you to identify the right stocks to invest in. You cannot just rely on mere guesswork. You have to take action and actually study the market if you want to make a large profit. Just like any other investment or business, investing in stocks also demands continuous research and practice. You need to learn and apply effective strategies. You also need to be flexible enough and be ready for abrupt changes in the market. All in all, participating in the stock market can be challenging, but it is nonetheless, very rewarding.

Investing in stocks is only for the rich

Although it is true that there are wealthy people who invest in stocks, it is also true that many stock traders and investors are 'low rollers' or the people who only have a few hundred or thousand dollars in their trading account. The thing is, it is very easy to enter the stock market. If you are of legal age, have an Internet connection and a decent computer, and if there is no legal restriction in your country, then you can easily start investing in stocks. What's more, you can do all of this from the comfort of your home.

In case you didn't know, a majority of the people who consider themselves to be stock investors are not rich. In fact, the reason why they invest in stocks is not because that they are already rich but because they want to become rich. Now, different stock brokers may have different requirements or guidelines, but most brokers will allow you to start investing in stocks even with just a hundred dollars in your account.

To be successful, you need to have special connections

Although it can be quite an advantage if you have some sort of special connections that can help you come up with a profitable investment decision, this is not always the case. Getting inside information can only be beneficial to a certain extent, but it does not guarantee any favorable outcome. It should also be noted that nobody can guarantee the direction that the market is going to take. There are so many things that can happen, and many of which are outside of anyone's control. Although it can be an advantage if you have some special connections, you can still invest in stocks successfully on your own.

Investing in stocks will make you an instant millionaire

It is true that investing in stocks can make you a millionaire, but do not think that it will be fast and easy. In fact, a percentage profit of 20% in a year is already considered good enough. If you want to earn more money, then you will have to invest a bigger amount of funds.

Investing in stocks is safe and risk-free

In any investment, there are always some risks involved. This is also true when you invest in stocks. Many people who invest in stocks without taking the time and effort to understand the market end up losing all their capital in the long run. Hence, before you make any investment in stocks, be sure that you understand how it works and that you have thoroughly researched the market.

Investing in stocks will only make you lose all your money

There are also people who believe that if you invest in stocks, you will only lose your money in the long run. Again, you have to understand that you should not approach the stock market as a gamble. If you take the time and effort to closely study the market and apply effective strategies, then you can significantly increase your chances of making a large profit. Remind yourself that this is an investment. Just like any other investments, there are risks involved, but there is also that one golden opportunity to make it big.

Risks

Let us now discuss the risks involved when you invest in stocks. It is important that you be aware of these so that you will know just what to expect.

- **Market risk**
  Market risk refers to the people. When you say that you invest in stocks, it does not mean that your only concern would be the stocks alone. Do not forget that stocks move because of people. Hence, it is also important that you learn how to understand people for you to know what direction that the market is going to take. Unfortunately, the market has its own preferences and prejudices. What is more, people can have different opinions. Indeed, it is not that easy to learn how to read the market and know how the people would respond to certain changes. It is possible that the best stock to invest in today may no longer be considered a profitable choice by tomorrow. This is because of the basic rule that people change, including their preferences. Hence, when you invest in stocks, it is important that you keep a close eye on the market and analyze how it moves and responds.

- **Economic risk**
  As already stated, the economy is one of the factors that affect the prices of stocks. In fact, the economy mirrors the situation of the stocks. Hence, if businesses and stocks are doing well, then the economy also improves. But, when the stocks and businesses are down, then this situation is reflected in the economy. Another challenging part is that there are certain things about the economy that is outside anyone's control. A good example of this would be the terrorist attack that took place in 2001. It made the economy suffer, and it resulted in a decrease in the prices of different stocks in the market. When this happens, you might be able to just ride out the bad streak, but there are times that the blow inflicted on the market is too great to recover from and leads to collapse.

- **Legal risk**
  This risk is mostly related to the relationship between the government and businesses. The government may enact laws that can affect the standing of businesses. There is the risk that the government might suddenly enact a law that can adversely affect a business. When this happens, and if the business concerned fails to handle it properly, then the prices of its stocks might drop. Laws may be enacted that can restrict or limit business practices. Of course, governments are not against businesses. After all, businesses are important to the economy. However, the government can enact laws to secure and protect the welfare of its people. Unfortunately, sometimes the exercise of this power and prerogative can adversely affect certain businesses.

- **Headline risk**
  This pertains to the risk of being negatively featured on the news. In a way, this functions like a negative promotion. This does not just refer to the traditional news, but anything that can go viral like social media. Because of the tight competition, some businesses resort to dishonest and unfair practices. If a negative promotion gains much attention, then it can influence the market, which is not good for a business. Of course, this can affect the price of its stocks in a negative way.

- **Commodity price risk**
  This refers to the risk in the price of certain commodities. Sometimes the prices of commodities change. Although this is good if the price increases, it is not good for businesses if it results in the price decreasing. It should also be noted that even if a company does not deal with the subject of commodities, it is still affected by this risk. This is because when the price of certain commodities change, then it also affects the purchasing power of the people. Needless to say, this can affect many other businesses, as well as their stocks. As you can see, this risk can affect the whole economy. As you already know, the economy has a close connection to the price of stocks.

- **Interest risk and inflation**
  For businesses that need financing, interest risk matters a lot. Of course, a higher rate would mean more problems for a business. As the rate that a business has to pay increases, it will be harder for it to stay in the game and make a profit for its own. Now, you can combine this with the risk of inflation. Combine these two, and you can find a trap that would be difficult for a business to get out of. Worse, if the economy also falls, then it would be almost impossible for any struggling business to survive.

Benefits

Now that you know the associated benefits of investing in stocks and if you think that you are still up for it, then it is time for you to know the wonderful benefits of investing in or trading stocks:

- **Profitable**
  Of course, the number one reason why people invest in stocks is because that it is a profitable investment. Although there are risks involved, once you get used to the market and develop a good understanding of how it works, then you can turn the stock market into a goldmine. In fact, there are people who have left their 8-hour office job and now invest in stocks as a full-time career. Indeed, if you get good at investing in stocks, then you can earn a high amount of profit from it.

- **Convenient**
  Thanks to modern technology, you can easily invest in stocks from the comfort of your own home. All you need is access to the Internet, and you can start using some trading platforms. Once you work as a stock investor, you can enjoy working while lying in bed, wearing nothing but your pajamas. Making trades and investments is also fast and simple, and all it takes is just a few clicks of the mouse.

- **You are the boss**
  If you are tired of always having to please your boss and doing whatever he or she tells you, then becoming a stock investor might just be the path for you. When you engage in stock investment, you become your own boss. You do not have to wake up early in the morning or do things you do not want to do. You take full control of everything. However, just be careful. As the saying goes, "With great power comes great responsibility." Just as you are the boss, you are also responsible for everything. If you get too lazy to study the market or become too careless, then the chances are that you might lose your investment. Still, you are the boss. Just be sure to be responsible enough so that you will not regret it.

- **Financial freedom**
  Indeed, there is no better way to obtain financial freedom than making money work for you. Normally, people work for money. However, successful investors know better. They know that the secret to financial freedom is to make money work for you instead. You can only do this by making an investment. Now, when it comes to investments, one of the best investments that you can make is putting your funds in profitable stocks and watching them grow. Indeed, becoming a successful stock investor is an excellent way to attain financial freedom. It is time for you to stop being a slave working for money. By becoming a stock investor, you can make money work for you.

- **It's fun**

    It cannot be denied that the activities of a stock investor can be really fun. In fact, many investors do not notice the time pass them by as they enjoy coming up with sound investment decisions. It can be fun to follow up on the market and find out if your last positions gained any profit. Of course, it is really nice and exciting every time you see that you have made a profit just by choosing the right stocks to invest in. You are not just your own boss, you can also be a highly successful person.

Stock trading broker

Before you can start investing in stocks, you need to open an account with a broker first. Now, by simply using your favorite search engine, you will find a long list of different brokers that offer the same service and allow you to invest in stocks. You need to choose the broker that will best suit your needs. More importantly, you need to work only with a trustworthy and reliable broker. Unfortunately, there are so many scammers and hackers online. So, how do you identify the broker that is right for you? Here are the criteria that you should consider:

Latest reviews

Before you deposit your hard-earned money into your account, be sure to check the latest reviews given to the stockbroker. You can do this easily by using your favorite browser. Simply type the name of the broker followed by the word 'reviews.' The 'Search Engine Result Pages' (SERP) will then show you related pages. Read as many reviews as you can and compare them with the reviews given to other brokers.

You should also pay attention to the dates when the reviews were made. If the last reviews were made about a year ago, then you should exercise more caution. Do not forget that the management team can change and how the broker handles its operations can also change. Also, it's worth keeping in mind that just because a broker has many positive reviews, that does not necessarily mean that you should no longer exercise caution when you're dealing with them. You should be diligent at all times. The positive reviews can only help to make you feel more confident about working with a broker, but it does not guarantee that the said broker will not scam or treat you unfairly. Always exercise caution.

Banking

Before you put money into your account, you should check the banking page or information of the broker first. It is not rare to find brokers that have more options for making a deposit and only a few limited options for making a withdrawal. Hence, before you deposit any money, be sure that you take note of the deposit and withdrawal methods acceptable to your broker. Otherwise, you run the risk of having your funds locked in your account without any way of withdrawing them. If this matter is not clear to you, do not hesitate to contact the customer support team.

It should also be noted that it is common for brokers to require certain documents, mostly documents that verify your identity, like a valid ID and billing statement before it processes a withdrawal request. Be sure that you have the required documents in your possession and that they have not yet expired. Most brokers are strict with the processing of withdrawals, so be sure that you understand this clearly.

Brokers normally restrict the withdrawal method to the deposit method that you use. For example, if you deposit via PayPal, then you should also withdraw your funds using PayPal. Of course, not all brokers have this limitation, so be sure to check it out before you make any substantial deposits into your account.

Trading or Investment platform

Of course, it is your broker that will provide you with the trading or investment platform that you will use to buy and sell stocks. The platform should make the experience of trading easy and convenient for you. It should also provide you with tools like graphs and other important data to help you come up with a sound investment decision. It should also be professionally designed. Although the design may not be considered by others to be necessary, it is still helpful as it helps set you in the right mood for investing. Again, the platform provided by your broker should help you make investments and give you a convenient experience.

Fees

Brokers may charge fees for certain transactions, such as a trading fee (which is a fee imposed per trade), surcharges, and withdrawal fees, among others. You should look for a reliable broker that charges the lowest rate possible. Although the fees may just be small amounts, they can easily pile up into a big amount. This is true, especially if you intend to make multiple trades in a week.

If you want to engage in day trading, then you can expect to make multiple trades in a day. Therefore, you should pay attention to the fees that are being charged by your broker. The fees may differ from broker to broker, so be sure to make a comparison. Needless to say, when it comes to choosing a broker, it would take much more than just finding out the one with the lowest fee. You should focus more on finding a reliable and trustworthy broker, a broker that will not rip you off and run away with your money. This is one of the reasons why you should only work with popular brokers who have positive reviews.

Minimum and maximum amount per investment

Knowing the minimum and maximum amount that you can invest is also important to know what kind of strategy that you should use. Knowing the minimum amount per investment or trade is also important especially if you are working on a low budget.

Mobile feature

These days, it is much more convenient to access the Internet using your mobile device. Brokers know about this, so they often come up with a mobile version of their platform. Do not worry, most, if not all, trustworthy brokers offer a mobile version that will allow you to make investments using your phone or tablet.

The mobile version may not allow you to access all the features of the site. This is normal. But, it should allow you to do important actions such as buying and selling stocks, as well as making a deposit or requesting for a withdrawal. A trading or investment platform with a mobile application is a must these days as it not only makes the process of investing in stocks more convenient, but it also allows you to invest in stocks virtually anywhere by just using your mobile device.

Customer support

When you work with a broker, especially if you intend to work with them for a long time, then it is strongly advised that you choose a broker that has an active and helpful customer support department. The customer support will help you with any technical issues that you may have with the site, as well as any other related questions that you might have in the future. Find out how to get in touch with the support team. Normally, there is a separate page on the platform where you can send customer support a message. Some brokers even provide a number that you can call, as well as an on-page chat feature, while others might only provide you with an email address. One way you can find out how helpful the customer support is by testing them. You can do this by sending an inquiry to the support team and check just how well it handles your inquiry. Normally, you should get a response from the support team within 24 hours.

Demo account

Most brokers will provide you with a demo account. Using a demo account is an excellent way to have a real market experience without risking any real money. Of course, you will also not earn any money from it, but it is a good and safe way to gain experience.

Even if you are already a well-experienced investor, you can still benefit from a demo account. A demo account can be helpful with testing your strategy in the market. After all, the life of a stock investor is mostly about developing your winning strategy. Having a demo account can save you from losing money as you look for that winning strategy.

Trading psychology

What is 'trading psychology?' Well, it simply refers to the mindset of a trader or investor. This is important since your mindset plays an important role in your success. You should be aware of the different mindsets, especially the ones that you should avoid to help minimize your risks and losses. Remember that your mindset is crucial to your success.

Greed

Greed is often the main reason why many investors lose their money. Although you invest in stocks to earn a profit, you should keep your desire under control. Investors lose their money not because they failed to pick the right stocks, but because they held on to those for too long. Do not forget that the stock market is volatile. This means that the prices of stocks are susceptible to change. They rise and fall continuously. You want to hold on to a position when the price is going up, and you must be disciplined enough to let go of it before the price drops.

Fear

This is the opposite of greed. Because of fear, investors fail to make good investments. Accept the fact that there will always be risks involved no matter how hard you study the market. It is your job to strike a balance between fear and greed. To combat fear, you need to gain more knowledge and learn how to apply an effective strategy.

Regret

Regret is when you miss out on a good investment. Do not worry, this is normal. Every time that you experience this, simply learn from the experience. Remember, there is always a lesson to be learned from the things we regret. This also happens when you commit a mistake and lose a position. Again, do not be discouraged. Simply learn from it. After all, you will surely commit mistakes every now and then. The important thing is to learn from your experience and use your knowledge to become a better investor. The more that you learn, the more profits that you can make.

Overconfidence

Although having confidence is good, too much confidence is a sure way to lose all of your money. Be sure to keep your confidence in check. A common mistake is to start doing less research after experiencing a series of profitable investments. Remember, don't ever let down your defenses. Instead, you should continue to work hard, if not harder. Always study the market, and never make any investment without sufficient research.

Winning mindset

The 'winning mindset' refers to a person who does not submit to fear or greed. An important part of having this winning mindset is to have self-discipline. Now, this may surprise you, but a person with a true winning mindset does not focus so much on the money. This is because someone with a winning mindset has already realized that money will come as long as you continue to make the right investment decisions. Instead of focusing on the money, focus on the facts and circumstances of the stock market. By doing so, you can increase your chances of choosing the right stocks to invest in.

A person with a winning mindset also knows that continuous success takes time, dedication, and effort. If you want to keep on making profits, then you should keep on working. Hence, you need to continue studying the stock market and develop a winning strategy.

You should also not panic even during a market collapse. Panicking will only lead to you making more wrong decisions. Instead, you should always be in control of your emotions. Don't submit to fear and panic. Learn to stop, relax, and view the market from a clear and calm perspective. This way you can come up with better decisions.

A person with a winning mindset also knows that in order to be successful, you need to take some risks. However, this is not just freely taking all kinds of risks but calculated risks. This refers to a risk that you can handle. A person with a winning mindset also knows how to handle losing trades or investments. After all, in the long course of making investments, it cannot be avoided that you will also encounter the bitterness of losing your positions. However, remember that what is important is not always winning every position that you have, but making a profit once you put everything together. A person with a winning mindset also knows the importance of positive thinking but remains reasonable and logical. They do not delude themselves and come up with practical solutions and actions. Last but not the least, a person with a winning mindset does not give up and always looks for ways to improve.

Building a winning mindset does not happen overnight. It is a result of continuous study and practice. Do not rush the development process, and try to learn as much as you can. Continue to improve yourself and be the best investor that you can be.

Chapter 2: Stock Trading Strategies

You cannot achieve a consistent flow of profits just by relying on luck. To significantly increase your chances of success, you should use effective strategies. Take note that just reading about these strategies is not enough. Investing in stocks is like learning a new skill. You also need to practice it. Let us discuss some of the notable strategies that you should know:

Fundamental analysis

Fundamental analysis is also referred to as the 'lifeblood' of investment. Hence, this is definitely something that is worth learning. This strategy does not just apply to the stock market but also in all kinds of investment. So, what is fundamental analysis? Fundamental analysis studies the fundamentals or the basics. As such, it is very important. You are probably familiar with the saying, "Knowledge is power." Well, this is what this strategy is all about. When you use this strategy, you should research and analyze the different factors that affect a stock or the stock market in general, such as the economy, level of competition, legalities, as well as market acceptance, among other things.

When you use this strategy, it is important that you follow up on the latest news since the news reveals important information about the stock market. Although fundamental analysis might be the strategy that demands the most time and effort, it is also highly effective. If you are serious about being a successful stock investor, then you should definitely learn about this strategy. In fact, successful investors use this daily. As a professional investor, you need to be up-to-date with the latest developments in the stock market.

It is also worth noting that fundamental analysis can be used along with another strategy. This strategy is not just about gathering all kinds of information. Rather, it has to be high-quality and reliable information. Of course, you also need to do your own analysis to identify the best information. You will soon realize that the more that you know about the market and the different stocks, the more likely it is that you will come up with the right investment decisions.

Technical analysis

If you are the visual type of person, then you might find this strategy interesting. Technical analysis makes use of graphs and charts to study the price movements of a particular stock. The idea behind this strategy is that the different factors that can affect a stock have their final effect on its price. Therefore, just by analyzing the price movements of a stock, you also get to deal with all the factors that influence it. You might want to consider this as the simplified and visual version of fundamental analysis.

When you use this strategy, you should learn to read patterns. Okay, you might be wondering: "Do patterns really exist?" The answer is 'yes.' In fact, even a random generator creates patterns. However, it should be noted that patterns come and go. What this means is, you cannot expect to see a pattern all of the time. There will be times when no matter how hard you study a graph, there is simply no pattern to be seen. Again, you don't need to worry because this is normal. A common mistake is forcing yourself to see a pattern even when no pattern exists. Remember, always make your analysis with a clear and unbiased mind. It is better for you not to proceed with making a decision than forcing yourself to see something which isn't even there.

Just like fundamental analysis, technical analysis can be used together with another strategy. In fact, many expert traders use both fundamental and technical analysis at the same time. Indeed, the more information that you have, the more likely it is that you can come up with the right investment decision. Technical analysis is an excellent strategy for short-term investments, but it can also be used for long-term investments.

Averaging down

This strategy will allow you to purchase stocks at a bargain. You can then sell them for profit. The best way to explain how this works is by using an example. Let us say, you want to buy the stocks of company X, and its current price is $10 per stock. You then make a buy order at the said rate. If its price increases, then you can easily sell it for profit. Now, if the price decreases, then according to this strategy, you should make another buy order. So, if the price drops, say, to $9, then you should make a buy order at $9. Now, if the price decreases again, then make another buy order at the lower price. This way you are buying stocks at a much lower price.

Okay, you might be wondering: "Are you not simply buying a losing stock?" Although it may look like it, this is not actually the case. In fact, you are making a sound investment. Just imagine how much profit you could make once the price of the stock goes back to its original price (its price when you first applied the strategy) or higher. All the buy orders that you have made will give you a nice return on your initial investment.

Now, it should be noted that this approach is considered highly aggressive, so be very careful every time you use it. The key here is to identify a stock that will most likely increase in price. Take as much time as you can to research the stock concerned, as your success will depend on whether its price will increase or at least recover in the near future.

A good strategy to use together with averaging down is fundamental analysis or technical analysis. You cannot use averaging down alone on its own as it relates only to the amount that you invest and does not tell you where to make an investment. Of course, where you put your money in is a crucial factor when it comes to making profitable investments. This strategy will allow you to weather fluctuations in the market since you're holding on to profitable stock investments. Again, keep in mind that although this seems highly practical, it is still considered a highly aggressive approach.

Growth investing

This is where you invest in the stocks of a company because you believe that the company has a potential to grow. This is usually used for small and start-up companies since they have room for development. When you use this strategy, take a look at new businesses. Consider how they are positioned in the market. Can they match up with the competition? Do not just focus on the company. Keep in mind that the strengths and weaknesses of a business are relative to the strengths and weaknesses of its competitors. Therefore, you should also keep an eye on competing businesses. This is a good way to gauge how a particular business is doing in the market. It is not enough that a company has space to grow, but the business should take positive actions to grow even further. Last but not the least, you should also pay attention to market acceptance. After all, no matter how amazing a business is, it would not do any good if the market ignores it or simply does not accept what it offers. These are the important things to consider when you use this strategy. The drawback of using this strategy is that since you will most likely be dealing with start-up companies, there may not be enough information that you could use to measure the profitability of these companies. This is a challenge that you have to overcome with this strategy.

Value investing

This is similar to growth investing. However, in this case, it is the value that you need to look into. When you use this strategy, you should look for a company that offers its stocks at a price that is lower than their actual value. Okay, this is where the challenge is. It is you who will have to determine the value of their stocks of the company. You need to look for stocks that are underpriced in the market. The idea behind this strategy is that the value of the stocks will soon adjust and correct itself. When this happens, and if you find a company that is underpriced, then you will soon gain a nice profit. Unlike growth investing, value investing does not just work on new companies. It can also apply to old companies or stocks. Still, this is a good strategy to use on new and start-up companies since they tend to have good value but have a low stock price. It is good to use this strategy together with fundamental analysis. Take as much time as you need to study the company. Of course, do not forget to compare its strengths and weaknesses with the strengths and weaknesses of its competitors. If you find a company that has good value but is underpriced, then that is an opportunity that you can take advantage of. When you use this approach, it is important that you should not be biased about anything. Always keep an open mind and do your best to understand the company before you make any real investment.

Stock split

In a 'stock split,' a stock is split, and so it gets divided. For example, if a stock or share costs $40. After a stock split, then you will end up with two stocks at $20 each. Take note that it does not always have to be an equal split. The point is that the stock will be divided, and so its price should also be divided accordingly. This is usually done by companies when the price of its shares gets too high. So, they move for a stock split to lower the price. This is also because investors tend to shy away from stocks that are too pricey. Now, this is actually a good sign. It usually means that the business is doing good. Normally, after a stock split, the price of stocks still continues to increase. When you use this strategy, you should pay attention to companies that just declared a stock split. This normally signifies that they're doing well.

Now, you should be careful. A common mistake is to fall for a reverse split. This is like a stock split, but it is not good. In a reverse split, stocks are combined, which causes the price of stocks to increase. Since there is an increase in price, it might look as if it were a good investment, although that is not really the case. Here is an example. Let us say that there are 10 stocks at $10 each. In case of a reverse split, then you will end up with five stocks at $20 each. This is the opposite of a reverse split. In this case, the price of stocks increases not because the company is doing well, but it's because of a manipulative action made by the company. Hence, do not forget that a simple increase in the price of stocks is not good enough of an indicator that the company is doing well.

Take note that, although a stock split is often a good indication that the company is doing well, you should still do your own research before you make an investment. A stock split alone is not enough. You should take a closer look at the company and study it carefully. This way you can increase the chances of making a good investment.

Stock mastery

The more that you know and understand a particular stock, the more likely that you can predict its price movement. This is the idea behind this strategy. When you use this approach, you should choose a particular stock that you like which you think is profitable. Your job is to make sure that you read and analyze the said stock every day. After some time, you will notice that since you know the said stock so well already, you can easily predict its behavior in the market, and this will allow you to take advantage of it and make a nice profit.

Read and find out as much as you can about your chosen stock. Now, it is also common that you might suddenly realize that the stock is not a profitable investment as you study it. This is well and good because it will help you lower your losses. In this case, do not be discouraged. Simply move to another stock and start over. Do not consider your efforts as a waste. If you end up with a losing stock, then be thankful for the fact that you have saved money by not making any real investment.

Once you gain mastery over a stock, then you can start taking advantage of it. But, how do you know if you have mastered a particular stock? There is no strict rule regarding this matter. The important thing is that you can predict its price movements correctly most of the time. Once you attain mastery over a particular stock, then feel free to master another stock. However, when you move to studying another stock, do not neglect the previous stock that you have already mastered. The more stocks that you get to master, the better chances you have of making a large profit. Do not rush the process of learning and researching information about a particular stock. Take note that you are aiming for mastery, and not just having mere knowledge of a stock.

Develop your own

As a professional investor, you can develop your own strategy. It can be as simple as making a few adjustments to the strategies that you already know, but you are also free to come up with an entirely new strategy of your own. The life of a full-time investor is mostly about developing a strategy. Keep in mind that the stock market is a continuously moving market. The strategy that you use should be up to date with the latest changes and developments. Therefore, as you work on your strategy, you should also keep a close eye on the stock market.

Developing your own strategy can take a long time. Be ready to go through some trial and error before you adopt a strategy and apply it using real money. This is a good time to make use of the demo account provided by your stockbroker so that you can test your strategy in a real market environment without risking any real money. If you do not want to make use of the demo account, then you can simply make small investments and see how they go.

Take note that strategies are highly sensitive. This means that even a minor change in your strategy can make a big difference. Therefore, when it comes to developing your own strategy, be sure to test it more than once even if you only have to make a small adjustment.

Chapter 3: Best Practices

Research

When it comes to choosing the right and profitable stocks to invest in, the important thing is to do your research. Remember, you should never make any investment without doing solid research. Now, it is true that many investors do their research and yet, still fail to pick the right investments. The reason why this happens is that many of these investors fail to render a sufficient amount of research.

So, just how much research is needed? There are no hard and fast rules on this matter, but you will know if it is enough once you can honestly say that you understand the stock that you intend to invest in, and that you also understand the present situation of the stock market.

This is also another reason why fundamental analysis is important. Indeed, if you are serious about doing well as an investor, then you need to do continuous research.

When you research a potential stock to invest in, you should make sure to gather quality information. Do not just limit yourself to the news, but also be open enough to consider what other investors think. There are many investors who write blog posts and articles. Although it's not required, it will also help if you take the time to consider their opinions. It is also advised that you join online groups and forums on the subject. This will not just allow you to meet people who share the same interest, but it is also a good way to learn interesting viewpoints, opportunities, and even new strategies. Again, remember to never make any investment if it is not backed up by a solid research. Otherwise, you will only end up gambling, and this is not the suggested approach since the risk of losing your investment is high if you do not conduct enough research.

Start small

It does not matter how much funds you have in your account. If you are just starting out, then it is strongly advised that you start out small. Your first objective is not to make money right away but to familiarize yourself with the trading environment. In fact, it is advised that you start out by using the demo account provided by your broker. Do not worry, once you are used to the actual market environment, and once you have a reliable strategy, then you can easily increase the amount of your investment. Again, do not rush the learning process. This can help to effectively minimize your losses.

Write a trading or investing journal

Although it's not a requirement, writing an investment journal can be very helpful, especially in the long run. You don't need to be a professional writer to come up with a journal. However, there are two things that you have to keep in mind:

- You should update your journal regularly
- You should be completely honest with everything that you write in your journal

So, what should you write in your journal? Well, you are free to write everything that is related to investing in stocks. After all, it is your journal, so feel free to do whatever you want with it. Ideally, your journal should contain your reasons for investing in stocks, your goals and objectives, the stocks that you are currently studying, lessons and mistakes, as well as your strategies, among other others.

Having a journal will allow you to view yourself from a different perspective, from a standpoint that is free from any form of bias and prejudice. As you can see, this is why it is important that you update your journal regularly and that you should be very honest.

In the first few weeks, you might not appreciate the benefits of having a journal. However, just continue writing your journal. After some time, you will start to appreciate its importance, especially once you notice your progress.

As you should already know, a journal is not just a notebook that you write in. Rather, it should serve as a mirror of yourself that will help you see your strengths and weaknesses. It will also reveal to you lessons that you would have otherwise, overlooked. Needless to say, you should read your journal from time to time. As you read, you should also make reflections. Try to learn as much as you can from your journal. Keep an open mind and be open to new ideas and realizations.

Cash out

There are investors who like to keep all their profits in their account. The reason for this is they want to increase their funds. After all, the bigger the funds, the bigger the potential profit. However, although there is nothing wrong with growing your funds, you should understand that making a withdrawal is also important. If you do not withdraw your profits, then it's no different from using a mere demo account. Also, cashing out is a simple yet effective way of minimizing your risks and losses. Take note that as long as your money is in your account, it will be continuously exposed to risks. You don't need to withdraw all of the profits when you cash out of course. If you want, you can simply withdraw just

20% of your total profits. The important thing is that you make a withdrawal and enjoy the fruits of your work.

Take a break

Although the activities of an investor can be fun, it can also be tiring, especially in the long run. Hence, do not hesitate to give yourself some time off and take a break every now and then. Now, when you take a break, do not be like other people who still worry about their investments. It is advised that you close down all your positions before you take a break. This way, you would not have to worry about anything. When you take a break, do not even think about your investments. This is the best time to relax and just have fun. Just enjoy your vacation or at least have a movie night at home. The important thing is that you relax as much as you can. Although, after taking your break, you are expected to work even harder. So, enjoy it as much as you can.

Continuous improvement

Just as the market continues to move, you should always strive for continuous improvement. Do not let this book or any other books put any limitation on you. Always do your best to improve. Even if you think that you already know enough about a particular stock, you should still try to learn more about it. There is no end to continuous improvement.

You should also expand your circle and meet other investors. This is a good way to develop your skills and learn interesting views and strategies. One way you can improve yourself is by making short-term goals. Do your best to meet these goals. For example, aiming for a small 3% gain if you are just starting out is good. You can then raise the bar as you get used to investing in the stock market.

Diversify your risks

Diversifying your risk is another strategy that you should observe. This is not new, but it is also followed in this business. You are probably familiar with the saying that you should never put all of your eggs in one basket. There is no strategy or amount of research that can guarantee the success of any investment. Of course, this does not mean that you should no longer do your research and study the market. However, you need to be ready just in case the worst happens. After all, there are so many things that can happen in the course of the investment. This is why it is important that you diversify your risks. When it comes to investing in stocks, you need to spread your investments by opening multiple positions. Do not gamble all your money in one trading position. By diversifying your risks, there is still a chance for you to end up making a profit even if you lose one of your positions. Now, a common mistake beginners make is taking some of their positions for granted. They think that since they will open multiple trades, they can still survive even if they make some bad investments. Although this may be true, it is wrong to take any position for granted. If you observe expert and successful investors, you will see just how careful they are before they enter into any position. Even though they always closely follow the market, they are very cautious about opening or closing a position. They do not allow themselves to be overcome by overconfidence. Instead, they keep up with the best practices and stick to their winning strategy. Again, learn to diversify your risks. Doing so can save you from sudden and unexpected changes in the market.

Professional approach

Most people start investing in stocks as a hobby. Although there is nothing wrong with this, it is not the suggested approach. The problem with investing in stocks as a hobby is that in the stock market, you often receive what you deserve. Hence, if you take it as a hobby, then expect to gain (or lose) something as a mere hobby. Do not expect to make continuous profits. Taking something as a mere hobby signifies lack of dedication and commitment. You can compare this with the long hours that professional investors spend studying the market, and yet they are still very careful every time that they make an investment. So, what should you do? Instead of thinking of it as a mere hobby, you should take a professional approach. If you are busy and know that you cannot give it as much time as you would, then just be a part-time trader. That way you do not have to open multiple positions regularly. The important thing is to emphasize and know that you are serious about it. Do not take it lightly but give it as much commitment, time, and effort as it deserves.

Chapter 4: Mistakes to Avoid

Chasing after your losses

In gambling, gamblers are often advised not to chase after their losses. However, the surprising truth is that even those who are well aware of this advice still continue to chase after their losses. How does this happen? Well, you need to understand how this works. So, what does it mean to chase after your losses? This normally happens after you experience a bad loss. We all have the tendency or desire to recover our losses. Since you have already given it time and effort, you still want to make a profit even if it's just small. However, to do this, you will usually have to invest a bigger amount of funds. This is where the problem comes in. The amount that you invest may be difficult for your total finances to handle. Again, remember that there is no amount of preparation that can guarantee the positive outcome of any investment. The problem here is, if you lose that position, then you will certainly end up with a loss so huge that there may not be any practical way to get back your losses.

So, what should you do? Instead of chasing after your losses, experts advise that you should chase after more profits. After all, in the course of your investing career, it is unavoidable that you will encounter a number of losing positions every now and then. This is normal. The important thing is that you make a profit once you combine everything. Chasing after your losses forces you to take an aggressive strategy, which is often not good. Although chasing your losses do not always end up in a negative outcome, it is just too risky. If you continue to chase your losses, then you will most probably end up losing more money in the long run because of its high-risk nature.

Using an untested strategy

This is a common, yet serious mistake committed by beginners. You should keep in mind that even minor changes in a strategy can have a strong overall impact on the effectiveness of the strategy. Remember, you should never use an untested strategy. Be sure to run multiple trials before you use it to make a real investment. A good way to do this is to take advantage of the demo account provided by your online stock broker. Now, it is unavoidable that you will soon have to make changes or slight adjustments to your strategy. Remember, for every adjustment that you make, be sure to run some trials before you use it with real money. It is easy to get lazy and be tempted to skip the testing stage, but that is a serious error. You should get used to testing your strategy, as it will be a normal part of your life as a trader as you continue to develop your winning strategy.

Relying completely on expert advice

As a beginner, there is nothing wrong with listening to the advice given by so-called 'experts.' Most beginners even have their favorite blogs that they visit every now and then. However, it should be noted that it is wrong to completely rely on the pieces of advice given by these 'experts.' The sad truth is that many of these so-called 'experts' are not even real experts. In today's world, it is fairly easy to make anyone look like an expert, especially when you harness the power of social media.

Since many of these 'experts' are not even real experts, relying on their advice can be a serious problem. You should also consider that even the real experts out there still commit mistakes from time to time. If you are serious about becoming a professional investor, then you need to develop your own understanding and view of the stock market.

Of course, you are free and even encouraged to listen to the views and pieces of advice given by other stock investors, but you should only treat them as they are: a mere advice or suggestion. You still hold the final say and have total control over your own investments. Even as a beginner, you should aim to develop your own understanding of the market. Otherwise, you might end up being controlled by others, and this is not good for you and your investments. Feel free to listen to others but always take their words and ideas with a grain of salt. Remember, in this line of business you are your own boss.

Taking weak trading positions

Another common pitfall to avoid is having weak positions. Sadly, many investors end up with weak investments or positions that will most likely result in a loss. This normally happens because they make investments even if they are not sure of their positions. Just because you have spent hours of serious research does not mean that you are now in the position to make a wise investment decision. As a professional investor, it should be considered normal for you to spend hours doing research and analysis of the different stocks in the market. Now, before you make any investment, you should ensure that your decisions are backed up by solid research. If you honestly do not feel confident about a certain investment, then do not make any investment. You are not obliged to enter any position, especially if you are not feeling uneasy about it. Instead of keeping weak positions, it is better for you not to keep any investment at all.

Being a victim of the 'pump and dump' scheme

This is another pitfall that beginners fall into. To understand how it works, you should know what a 'pump and dump' scheme is. It is a fraudulent scheme. In a pump and dump scheme, the people behind it pump a particular stock by using promotional hype. It will appear as if a certain stock is a good investment. In today's world, it is very easy to promote and share information via the Internet. Once people believe that a particular stock is a good investment, they put money into it. Now, this will make the price of the said stock increase. This is the pumping stage. As the price increases, the more it will convince other investors to make an investment.

This is where the trick comes in. Once the price of the stock reaches a certain amount or when the people recognize that it is already overpriced for its real value, then the ones behind the scheme make a sell order. As a result, the fraudsters make a profit by selling it at a higher price. This is the dumping stage. Now, the drawback here is that its price will now fall, and those who are holding on to these stocks will end up with stocks that have a steadily declining price.

This is another reason why it is important for you to have your own understanding of the stock market. If you just listen to what other people tell you, then you will most likely end up as a victim of the pump and dump scheme. Yes, this fraudulent scheme happens in the real stock market, so you should be aware and exercise caution in your dealings.

Trading aggressively

Another mistake to avoid is being too aggressive. Now, being too aggressive might yield a higher profit, but it is also a quick way to lose your money. It is quite tempting to take the aggressive approach because it offers a higher return but it is also very risky to the point that if you keep on following this approach, then there is a good chance that you will soon lose your money. If you are just starting out, it is strongly advised that you stay away from any aggressive strategies. Or, if you have to be aggressive in any way, then be sure to control it and minimize the aggressiveness. Instead, you should focus on increasing your rate of success. You can do this by developing your winning strategy.

Learn to minimize your losses by minimizing your risks. Make sure that every trading position you enter is one you studied well and is backed up by research. Be conservative as possible. This does not mean that you should no longer focus on making a profit, you just have to avoid taking an extreme measure to gain a significant profit. Keep in mind that there is no end to investing, so you do not have to hurry. The stock market is always open, and it will continue to function no matter what. So, do not be impatient. Instead, keep an eye on available opportunities and be sure to grab them when they present themselves. Instead of focusing too much on the money that you want to make, focus on increasing your rate of success by always studying the stock market.

Conclusion

Thanks for making it through to the end of this book. We hope it was informative and that it provided you with all of the tools you need to achieve your goals whatever they may be.

The next step is to apply everything that you have learned. Investing in the stock market can be an interesting journey. Be ready to face some challenges along the way. The important thing is to keep on learning. Take note that to learn the strategies in this book, you have to practice them. Investing in stocks is just like learning a new skill. It does take some time and effort, but it is very much worth it. Again, do not rush the development process. The more that you learn, the more that you can minimize your losses and increase your profits.

If you want to achieve financial freedom or simply want to increase your income, then this book is for you. Investing in stocks can be challenging, but it is full of rewards for those who take the time and effort to learn it. There are people out there who earn their full-time income simply by investing in stocks. If you want a successful life by being your own boss, then give this wonderful opportunity a try.

Feel free to review this book and make your own reflections and modifications. Remember, you are dealing with a live and continuously moving market, so it is only right that you always strive for continuous improvement. This book has given you the tools to achieve total financial freedom. It is up to you to turn your newfound knowledge into actual practice. Finally, if you found this book useful in any way, a review on Amazon is always appreciated!

Description

Stock Market Investing for Beginners: Essentials to Start Investing Successfully is the ultimate guide that will teach you the ins and outs of investing in the stock market. This book unveils the secrets that will show you how you can successfully turn the stock market into your own personal goldmine.

Learn:

- What a 'stock' is
- What the stock market is
- Investing vs. gambling
- The truth behind the myths
- Risks and benefits
- What to look for in a stockbroker
- Trading psychology
- Powerful strategies
- Best practices
- Common mistakes to avoid

And so much more!

What's in the book?

- Chapter 1 discusses the basics. Learn about what a stock is and the stock market, among many others. This chapter will give you the foundation that you need to be successful

- Chapter 2 teaches the powerful stock investing and trading strategies that you can use to turn the odds in your favor

- Chapter 3 lays down the best practices that you should observe to increase your chances of making a profit

- Chapter 4 talks about the mistakes that you should avoid. You should take note of these pitfalls to avoid committing the same mistakes many other people have

www.ingramcontent.com/pod-product-compliance
Lightning Source LLC
Chambersburg PA
CBHW031517210526
45464CB00007B/2951